The Wanderer's Lust

The Wanderer's Lust is not just a collection of poems. It is, in many ways, a journal without dates — an emotional cartography of a soul that never stopped walking.

Each piece in this series was born from a moment — some fleeting, some haunting, some hopeful. But all of them were true. Not in the factual sense, but in the way they echoed something honest inside me. The Wanderer is not just a character. He is every one of us who has ever longed for something undefined. Who has loved without understanding why. Who has kept moving not to escape, but to feel.

This journey began as a whisper — a desire to give shape to silence. What unfolded was a path of 25 moments, threaded together by dust, memory, ache, and joy. It was never about a destination. It was about the act of walking, again and again, with nothing but a restless heart and a quiet kind of courage.

If you find a part of yourself in these words — even just a flicker — then the Wanderer has done his job. Because in the end, we are all wanderers. All searching. All becoming.

Thank you for walking with me.

Prologue: The First Step

He did not begin with a map.
He began with a whisper.

A pulse in his bones,
A question in his chest—

What if there is more?

And so he walked.

Not to escape,
But to remember.
Not to find,
But to feel.

This is not a tale of destinations.
This is the story
Of motion,
Of memory,
Of lust—

Not for love.
Not for land.
But for the wild ache of living.

He was not lost.

He was only beginning.

The Awakening (Poems 1–5)
The Wanderer's Lust - 1

He is no longer guided by ideals—
The Wanderer moves,
Not with purpose, but with fire.

His lust is not for flesh alone,
But for the unknown,
For more than life dares offer.

What once sated
Now bores him—
Old pleasures turn to dust.

His hunger
Knows no end,
His thirst grows with each taste.

So he walks,
Driven by a craving
No map can chart.

Each conquest behind him
Feeds the silence ahead—
And still, he yearns.

Beyond the edge of reason,
Beyond every fading star,
The Wanderer's Lust endures.

The Awakening (Poems 1–5)
The Wanderer's Lust – 2

There are things he
Wants, needs, wishes for—
Dreams that whisper through restless nights.
For most, desires shift with time,
But his remains unchanged—
The road forever calls his name.

Each step births a new beginning,
New places, new skies,
New thoughts sprouting like wildflowers
In the soil of his solitude.

He seeks no end, no final stop—
His destiny is not a point on a map,
But a trail of becoming.
His lust is not for land,
But for motion itself.

They call him a fool—
A drifter with no plan.
Children toss pebbles at his back,
Laughing at the dust he stirs.

But undaunted, he walks on,
For the road understands
What the world never could—
That some souls are born
To wander, not arrive.

The Awakening (Poems 1–5)
The Wanderer's Lust – 3

Where is he going?
Even he does not know.
One foot in front of the other—
The road decides, not he.

He no longer seeks a purpose,
Nor questions the why.
He belongs to motion now,
To wind, to dust, to sky.

Each path—smooth or broken—
Welcomes him the same.
He walks through thunder or stillness,
And never curses the rain.

He is not lost—
Only tuned to another rhythm,
Where maps are meaningless,
And silence speaks.

The world unfolds like a whispered prayer:
Colors bleed into memory,
Scents rise like ghosts,
And even the air hums with story.

He soaks it all—
Not to possess,
But to feel.

And in the hush between steps,
In the ache between stars,
Burns the only compass he trusts:
The Wanderer's Lust.

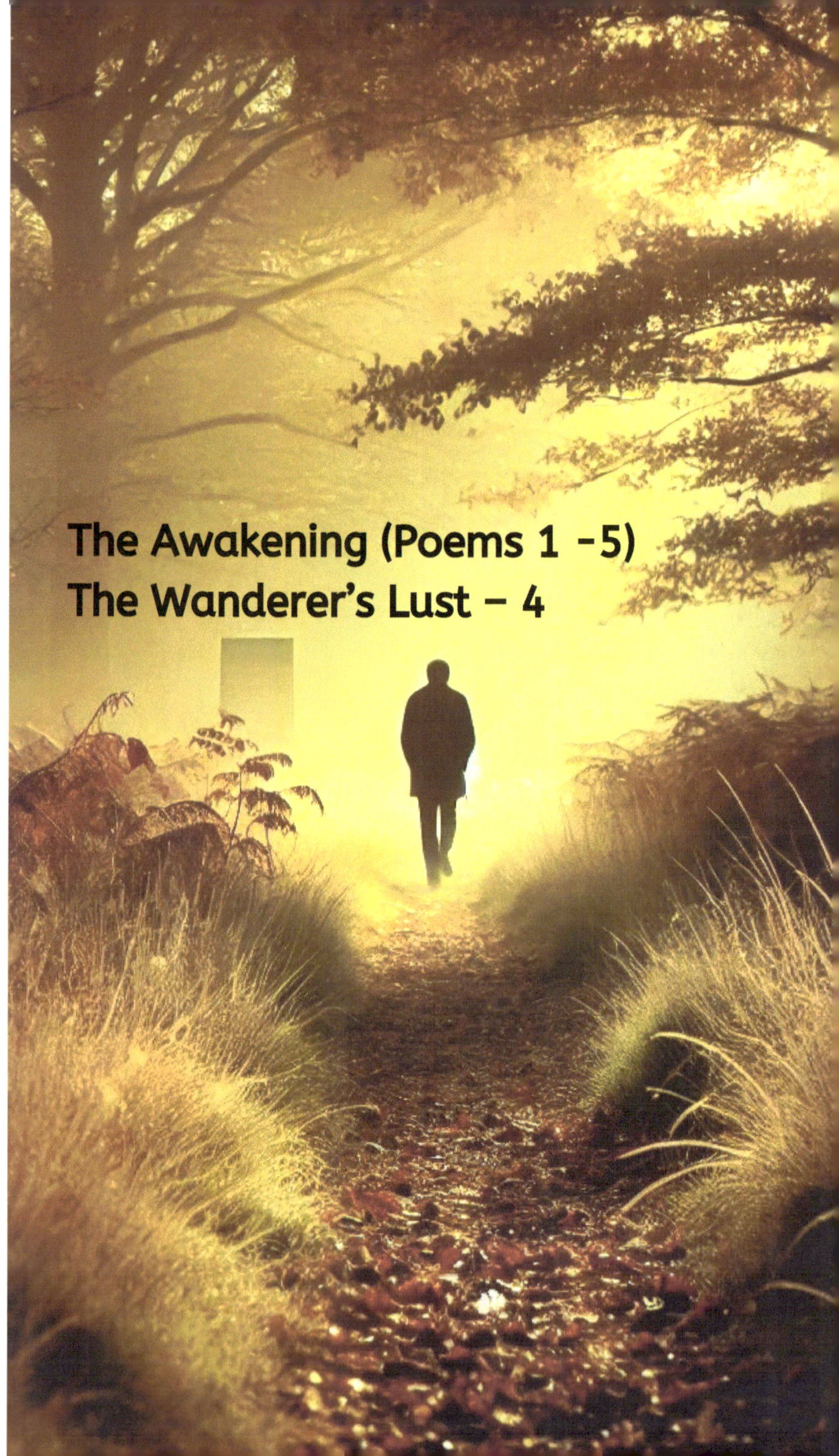
The Awakening (Poems 1 -5)
The Wanderer's Lust – 4

The crackle of leaves beneath his feet,
Or the soft grass cushioning his gait—
He notices, he absorbs... he forgets.

Each day begins a new becoming:
Frost that makes him slip,
Hay that gently breaks the fall.

He chooses to forget his paths,
So he can taste the now
In its raw, unfiltered fullness.

His wandering holds no consequence—
No destination, no applause.
Yet in each step, he breathes meaning.

This is his compass,
His truth unspoken—
Not lust for places,
But a lust for life.

The Awakening (Poems 1–5)
The Wanderer's Lust – 5

One cannot be joyous all the time—
Brimming with light,
Dancing through days.
Even the flame must flicker.

So it is with the Wanderer.
Beneath the shade of a tree,
He rests his tired body—
The road still humming in his bones.

He closes his eyes... but
The moment he does,
The indelible past comes rushing in.

Faces. Places.
Regrets like shadows
Stirring in his sleep.

With a shudder, he rises.
He must keep moving—
For if he stays too long,
The angels of his past
Will devour him whole.

II. The Becoming (Poems 6–10)
The Wanderer's Lust – 6

A catalyst is always required—
To turn life upside down,
And give it meaning anew.

What he believed in—shattered.
What he lived by—lost.
What he is now... different.

It is a quiet mutation,
A soft shedding of skin.
The Wanderer remains,
But the world around him—
Or perhaps within him—has changed.

He sees the same skies,
The same roads,
But everything feels unfamiliar.

Emotions no longer rage.
There is no fire to tame.
In his lust,
He has found something rarer—
A strange and steady contentment.

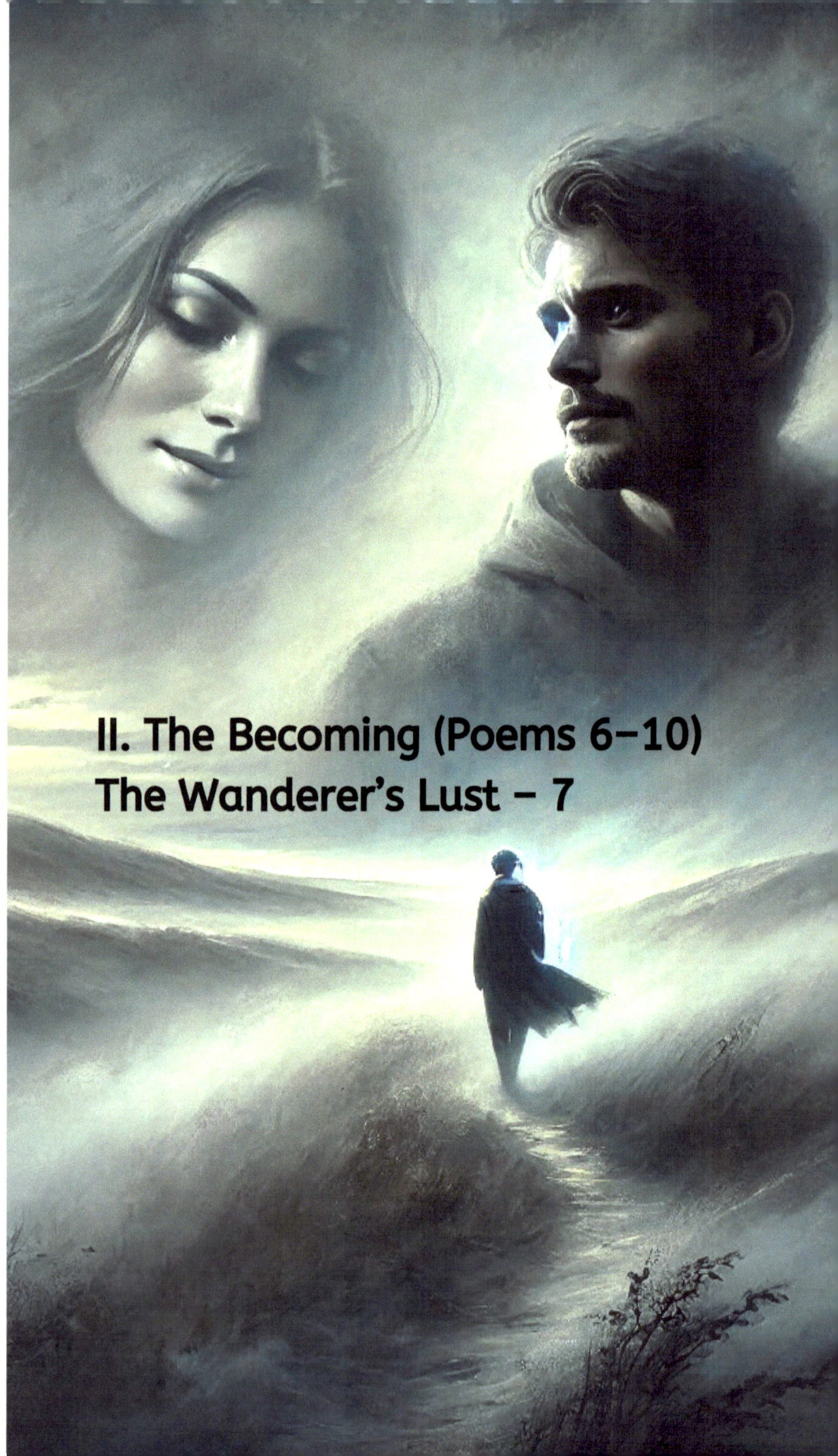
II. The Becoming (Poems 6–10)
The Wanderer's Lust – 7

The Wanderer is an addict.
Once, the addiction was change itself—
New skies, new scents, new winds.

Then he met you.

"What if I become your addiction?"
You said that—
And vanished into oblivion.

Now he wanders,
Not just for places—
But for the places that feel like you.

He searches for those oblivions
That cracked open his life.
"Am I not enough?"
He still hears the echo.

But the answer is buried
In the way he seeks you—
Everywhere,
In everything.

His lust no longer feeds on motion alone,
But on memory—
On the curve of your voice,
On the contentment
He once found
In the smile of your eyes.

II. The Becoming (Poems 6–10)
The Wanderer's Lust – 8

"Why do you walk the same path?"
They ask him.
"Don't you ever get bored?"

But the Wanderer is a child at heart.
His curiosity—untamed,
Unspoiled by the weight of oughts
And shoulds.

He thirsts.
He searches.
And somehow, he finds—
New wonders
In old roads.

Where others see repetition,
He sees revelation.
The same tree,
The same stone,
But always a new angle of light.

He takes joy
Not in novelty alone—
But in the way the familiar
Can surprise.

It is all the same...
Yet, beautifully,
Unpredictably,
Different.

II. The Becoming (Poems 6–10)
The Wanderer's Lust – 9

Everything comes to an end—
Even the grandest destinations
Fade into the rearview of memory.

But the journey...
The journey never ends.

So it is with the Wanderer.
He leaps from one dream to the next—
Lives it fully,
Then lets it go.

He carries no past,
And claims no future.
The present is all he trusts—
The heartbeat of now.

His lust for life
Is not a quest for victory,
Nor a race toward joy.

There are no wins or losses here.
Just motion.
Just breath.

And happiness—
Happiness without a reason.

II. The Becoming (Poems 6–10)
The Wanderer's Lust – 10

Something happens—
A word, a memory,
And he erupts—
In ecstasy...
Or sinks into a stupor.

He climbs mountains,
Drunk on delight.
He finds corners,
Shadowed and silent,
Where sorrow makes its nest.

Blanketed by his doom,
He broods, unmoving.
Then suddenly—
One fine day,
He's no longer who he was.
Different then,
Different now.

His voyage was never just about the world.
It was always him—
Turning inward.

For the Wanderer,
The greatest discovery is not you—
But himself.
And perhaps, when he finds that...
He will find you too.

III. THE HEARTSTORM (POEMS 11–15)
THE WANDERER'S LUST – 11

Once in a while,
The unexpected happens—
A turn, a glimmer,
A path not yet tread.

The Wanderer is a private soul.
He does not speak of his demons.
What lies within...
Stays within.

But once,
He stepped onto a path
That changed him.

He opened the doors he had sealed for years.
And she walked in—
Not to judge,
But to let the darkness fly.

It was a revelation.
He became vulnerable—
And in that rawness,
She became his mirror.

He thought he had nothing to learn.
But she showed him
How to feel without fear.

III. THE HEARTSTORM (POEMS 11–15)
THE WANDERER'S LUST – 12

Words have a way of weaving—
Soft threads in silence,
Spinning a story never spoken.

The Wanderer's language
Is not always written in ink—
But etched in glances,
In pauses,
In the ache between breaths.

His words live in emotion,
And the feelings they stir
Are never quite the same.

He leads others gently—
Down paths they didn't know they
remembered,
Until they feel something
They can't name.

Few walk the way he walks.
Fewer still feel what he feels.
His is a path of felt things—
Of quiet storms,
And a lust for life
That lives in every syllable.

III. THE HEARTSTORM (POEMS 11–15)
THE WANDERER'S LUST – 13

Every word spoken
Can alter the course of a life—
Especially when spoken
By someone you love.

But the Wanderer pretends not to care.
He shows no emotion.
He just walks.

He calls himself selfish.
Greedy.
Always wanting more.

He appears content—
A calm surface on still water.
But peel back the layers...

And you'll see it.

That hidden fire,
That aching truth—
His lust,
Not for the world,
But for you.

III. THE HEARTSTORM (POEMS 11–15)
THE WANDERER'S LUST – 14

There he goes again—
Overthinking.
Weighing shadows,
Wrestling ghosts.

Wondering what is,
And what might only be...
Air shaped like fear.

The silence of the road,
Soothing to some,
To him—
It stirs a storm.

It speaks in riddles.
It loops in echoes.
And the Wanderer begins to assume
What was never said.

The noise of the silence
Clouds his thoughts.
Everything—
Blurs.
Fogs.
Slows.

He tries to sweep away
The cobwebs of stillness,
To breathe light into the gloom.

But he fails.
And so,
Blinded by the fog within,
He walks on.

III. THE HEARTSTORM (POEMS 11–15)
THE WANDERER'S LUST – 15

The shadow of the past
Follows him—
A silent echo on the road,
A weight he cannot shake.

It clings,
Reminding him
Of where he began—
Of who he once was.

And ahead,
An apparition—
Shimmering, uncertain,
Beckoning him forward.

A future not promised,
But bright in its mystery.

His feet remain grounded.
But which way to lean?
Toward the pull of memory,
Or the whisper of becoming?

He must choose.
He must let go.

For only in surrender—
Can he truly soak
In the lust
Of the present.

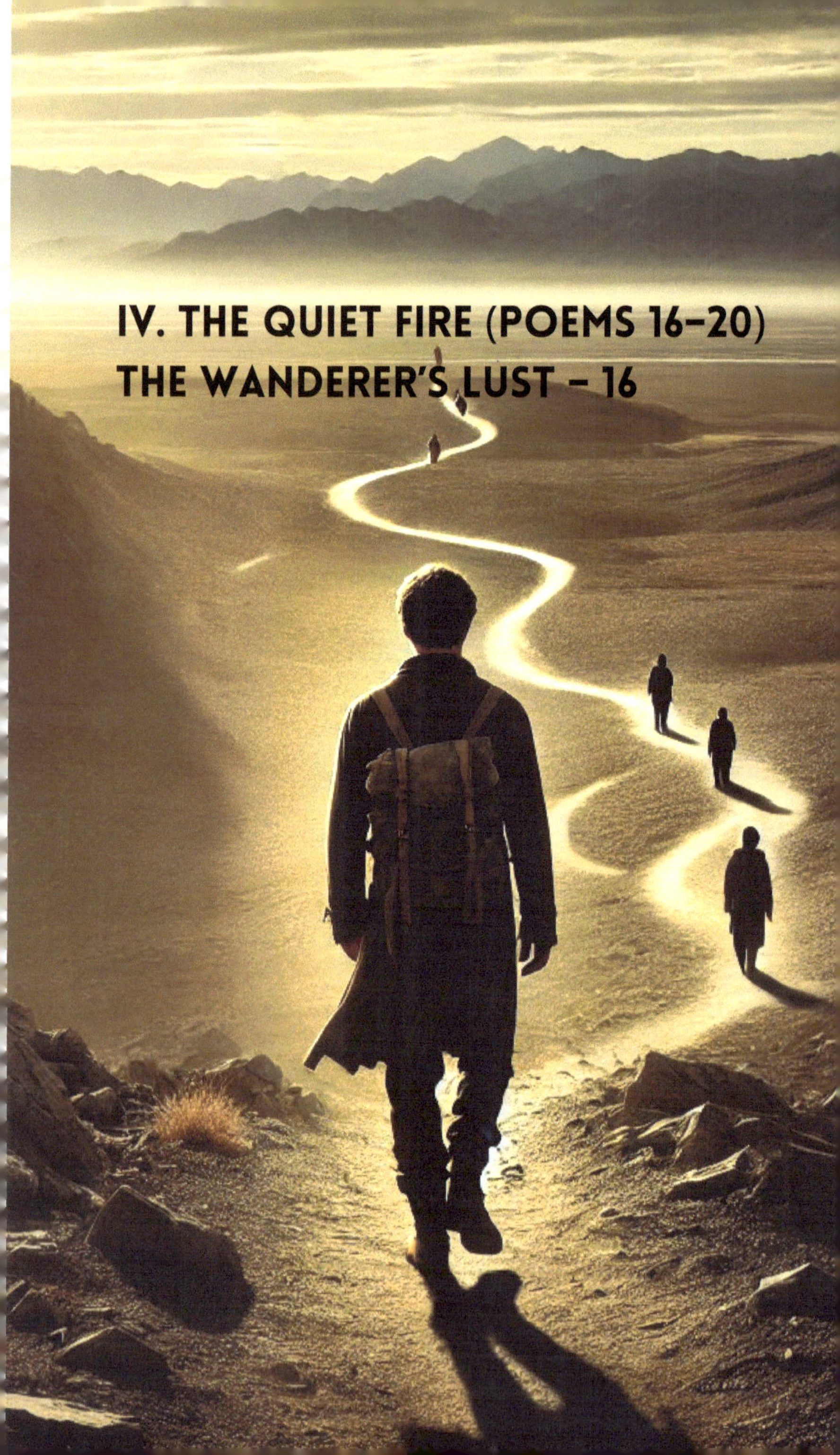
IV. THE QUIET FIRE (POEMS 16–20)
THE WANDERER'S LUST – 16

Everyone walks their own path—
Each journey,
A world unto itself.

To compare is to curse.
That's when greed creeps in.
Anger follows.
Jealousy waits at every bend.

The Wanderer has seen it happen—
His steps tangled with theirs,
With hers, with yours.

So now,
He closes his eyes.

His lust is his alone.
Unbothered.
Unhindered.
He travels.

He stumbles.
He falls.
He bleeds.
But he rises—
Smiling, even if blindly.

Because in the end,
He only wants
His journey
To be his own.

IV. THE QUIET FIRE (POEMS 16–20)
THE WANDERER'S LUST – 17

He is a walking ghost—
Haunted by demons
Born from experience,
Dragging him down
Into quiet pits of despair.

But there are angels, too.
Tiny wings,
Delicate flutters,
Weaving strings of smiles
Into the gray.

They lift him—
Gentle and unseen—
Placing him on clouds
Of stolen joy.

Euphoria, fleeting and bright,
Known only to him
And the beating of his heart.

Then—he falls.
Back to the ground.
Back to weight and duty.

But in the fall,
He gathers strength.
And with dust in his mouth,
He carries on.

IV. THE QUIET FIRE (POEMS 16–20)
THE WANDERER'S LUST – 18

He knows the path is lonely.
A dreamer rarely finds company—
For the world calls madness
What it cannot understand.

His lust to bring dreams to life
Comes at a cost—
Not to others,
But to himself.

Sleepless nights,
Empty echoes,
Endless miles
Chasing what only he can see.

His mission,
His vision—
All meaningless,
Until they succeed.

Then they will come.
They will gather.
They will sing his name.

They will hail the Wanderer.
But by then,
He will already be gone.

Still walking.
Still alone.
Still chasing the horizon
Only he can see.

IV. THE QUIET FIRE (POEMS 16–20)
THE WANDERER'S LUST – 19

He is stuck in time—
Wandering through paths
That lead to nowhere,
Or somewhere he cannot name.

Sometimes,
He carves his own way—
Cutting through jungle-thoughts,
Decoding the maze
Called life.

A glimmer of hope flickers here,
Another there.
Each spark reveals a layer of self—
Just as another layer forms.

For every truth uncovered,
A new question emerges.
He is peeling, unfolding,
Becoming.

In the darkness,
There must be light—
Somewhere.

In a world of lies,
In a forest of deception,
He walks on.

Because his lust for life
Still believes
There is truth
Waiting to be found.

IV. THE QUIET FIRE (POEMS 16–20)
THE WANDERER'S LUST – 20

Unseen.
Unknown to the world—
They met.

Like the banks of a river—
Always beside,
Never quite touching.

But there is only one destination
For this journey.
And it ends
At the spot where you stand.

He watches the riverbanks—
You and him.
Forever near,
But never meeting
In the eyes of the world.

Yet dive deeper...
Beyond the noise,
Beyond the trivialities of life—

And you'll see:

At the riverbed,
Where silence lives,
They are not two.
They are one.

V. THE SURRENDER (POEMS 21–25)
THE WANDERER'S LUST – 21

Many times along the way,
He crosses forests,
And deserts—
Barren lands,
Sans fruit, sans seed.

Hungry, tired,
Weathered by the journey,
The circle of life
Always brings him
Back to your village.

He knocks
At that all-too-familiar door.
You open it—
And in your gaze,
He radiates.

His hunger—
For warmth, for belonging—
Is momentarily
Satiated.

You see his happiness.
You feel it flicker
In your chest.

But the fetters of the world—
Expectations, fears,
Invisible walls—
Keep you from
Inviting him
To your heart,
His only home.

V. THE SURRENDER (POEMS 21–25)
THE WANDERER'S LUST – 22

Many grow weary in their travels—
Walking the same roads,
Tracing the same steps.
For them, monotony sets in
Like dust on tired shoes.

But the Wanderer is different.

He finds new ways
Of doing the same things.
His perspective shifts
With the wind,
With the moment.

No sunrise ever repeats itself.
The path may be familiar,
But never the mood,
Never the feeling.

And that—
That is what keeps him alive.

The colors shift.
The sounds change.
Even silence wears
A different face.

He walks the same path,
Yes—
But with each step,
Life becomes
Something entirely new.

V. THE SURRENDER (POEMS 21–25)
THE WANDERER'S LUST – 23

She wanders
Constantly
Through the corridors of his thoughts.

His addiction—
That's what she is.
Appearing in his desires,
Waking in his wishes.

He knows
That no addiction is ever good.
But the truth lingers—
Once an addict,
Always an addict.

She is the one
Who brings a smile
When no one else can.

She is the stillness
That quiets his storms.

He loses himself,
Again and again,
On dark, deserted paths.

And in those shadows,
It is only her
Who lights the way.

V. THE SURRENDER (POEMS 21–25)
THE WANDERER'S LUST – 24

The Wanderer was—
As unpredictable as an earthquake,
Volatile as a volcano's cry,
Raging like a forest set aflame.

He swam against streams,
Flew across the wind,
Met cliffs head-on—
And free-fell
Without fear.

Then came one night—
Intoxicated by presence,
By her—
And something shifted.

He was no longer a nomad,
No longer chasing nothing.
He became
A wanderer in her life.

Now,
He does not speak much.
His silence
Has become his language.

Not emptiness—
But the beautiful,
Unruly chaos
Of happiness.

V. THE SURRENDER (POEMS 21–25)
THE WANDERER'S LUST – 25

The Wanderer never gives up,
Never gives in—
Not on the things,
Not on the people
He believes in.
He loves,
Even when it hurts.

He would walk
All the miles the earth could stretch—
Even knowing
She would never be
At the destination.

A destination
Called the destiny of forever.
She was never meant
To be his ending.

But still—
She is his destiny.
Not to have,
But to be shaped by.

She lit his path
With a thousand small smiles—
And that
Was enough
To carry him
All the way.

Epilogue: The Last Step

He is still walking.
Not with the fire he once carried,
But with something softer—
A flame that does not burn,
But warms.

He has learned that not all longing is meant
to be fulfilled.
Some are meant to transform.

He no longer asks where the path leads.
He simply walks.

With her in his memory,
With truth in his silence,
With joy in his dust.

The Wanderer's Lust is not over.

It never needed to be

He walks not to arrive, but to feel.
Through forests of memory, deserts of desire, and skies of
silent longing, The Wanderer's Lust is a 25-part poetic
journey through solitude, love, loss, and awakening.

This is not a story of destinations.
It is a map of the inner terrain —
where dust speaks, silence guides,
and even longing becomes light.

For those who have ever ached for something more,
for those who carry invisible roads inside them—this
collection is your companion.

Step in.
Walk slow.
Feel everything.

9 798889 777527 9